# Verses from a Garden, and other nature things

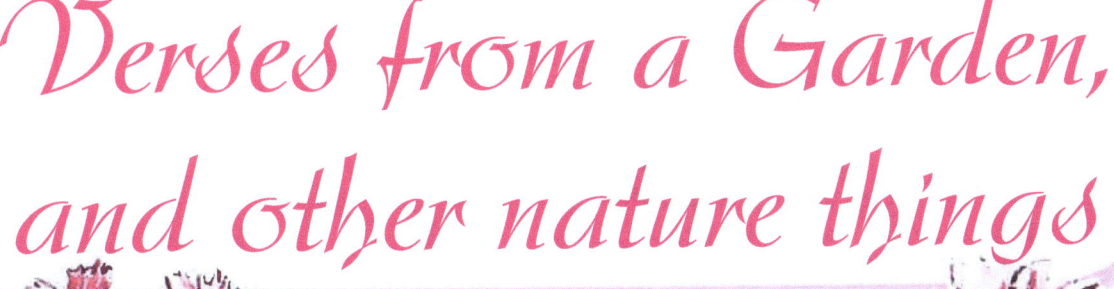

Carol Joan Campbell

Inks and Bindings
888-290-5218
www.inksandbindings.com
orders@inksandbindings.com

4

# GARDEN PICTURES

Our garden is a picture book,
All filled with colors bright.
I think that Mother Nature
Spreads new colors every night.

She painted all the roses in
Yellow, pink and red.
Then spilled a little over on
Miss Carnation's head.

The little Bachelor Buttons
She made the brightest blue,
Then she brushed the Forget-Me-Nots
And they were painted too.

The red and blue then blended
Into violets purple hues -
There just can't be a favorite,
I could never ever choose.

6.

# FRANNY FERN

Well, hello Miss Fern! I see your bowed head
As you come up from under the ground.
Are you looking for friends like Miss Violet
As you gently turn round and around?

Perhaps when you see her, you call out in joy
In voices so soft we can't hear,
And say, "Oh good day, I've been waiting for you -
Let's have a new, wonderful year."

Then together you grow on the soft forest floor;
You get taller and bigger and full,
And Miss Violets family grows bigger each day,
Making small purple dots down below.

# RUSTY, OUR DOG

Dad and I went for a walk in the woods
One day in earliest spring.
The ground was still covered with soggy brown leaves,
But the spring birds were starting to sing.

Our doggie Rusty was chasing squirrels he heard
And ran back and forth oh so fast,
He'd run to one side, and then far behind,
But then he'd race on and go past.

We laughed and threw sticks so he'd chase them and jump,
Then he'd fetch them to bring back for us.
He had such a good time, but we had to go home -
I knew when Mom saw muddy paws, she would fuss.

When we come back in summer, all we'll see is green
From the grass to the tree tops so high.
But it will be shaded and lovely and cool
And we'll love it, dear Rusty and I.

# PRETTY PANSIES

I looked right at some pansies
And they looked back at me.
They had little faces
Just as pretty as could be.

I know of people black and white,
Some red and yellow too,
But I've never seen a purple face -
Or yellow fringed in blue.

They seemed to be a little sad
Because they couldn't play,
'Cause they were firmly planted
In our garden in some way.

I found they did a little dance
When Mr. Breeze flew by -
They fluttered and they curtsied,
Then they looked up at the sky.

I clapped for them and thanked them
For the lovely show I'd seen,
And I think that they smiled back,
Or was that just a dream?

# ROSES

I sat out by the garden and closed my eyes real tight.
That shut out all the sunshine and made it seem like night.

It was then I really noticed something smelled good by my nose,
And I knew without peeking, the sweet scent of a rose.

I opened up my eyes and touched the petal that was smooth,
And saw the perfect color just as red as Mama's rouge.

Then I began to wonder if the rose was feeling me,
And if indeed it smelled me too; do you think that this could be?

I wondered if it said "Aha, I smell a child is near",
And if it may just be afraid that I might pick it here?

Perhaps that's why it has it's thorns, to keep small hands away;
So it can just grow on the bush, right where it wants to stay.

14

# PICNIC TIME

I think that a picnic's a best of all treat
With such wonderful goodies all packed up to eat.
We find a nice place where the grass is all green
And spread out a cloth that's all fresh and clean.

Then we run and play games like hide and go seek
Until finally it's time to sit down and eat.
Oh to open the basket and find what's inside -
Sandwiches, salads and chicken that's fried.

I know when that's finished, there still will be more,
Like fruits, watermelon, or cookies in store.
Picnics are special, even Moms and Dads say
Nothing can be better on a warm summer day.

# A GARDEN WEDDING

My Mommy took some Holly Hocks,
Some big flowers, and buds too.
Then she took some toothpicks
And told me what to do.

I turned a white flower over
So it sat firmly on the ground -
Then I put a toothpick in a bud
And turned that upside down.

Now I put them both together
And saw, with lots of pride,
I'd made a special "person"
Who looked just like a bride.

I followed now with pink and red
And couldn't help but smile,
As it looked like lots of bridesmaids
All walking down an aisle.

Mommy laughed and joined me
As we made our ladies march,
Then she took some twigs
And formed them into a tiny arch.

Now we moved all of the ladies through
And hummed a little tune.
Oh we had a gorgeous wedding
On this lovely day in June.

# DRAGON STORM

There's a dragon storm a'comin,
I can see it in the sky.
He's puffing out some black smoke clouds,
And soon they'll start to cry.

When the dragon gets all angry
He spits out bolts of fire!
And then he roars and bumps the clouds
When he flies ever higher.

The only thing to "gentle" him
At times is yet to come,
For he always seems to disappear
When he sees Mister Sun.

# MAMA ROBIN

I wonder what the Robin thinks
While sitting in her nest?
I wonder if she's choosing names
To see which sound the best?

Indeed it must be boresome
Just warming up those eggs -
You'd think she'd need some exercise
For body, wings and legs.

I wonder if she counts the days,
The hours and the minutes -
And if she calls for Daddy
To take his own turn in it?

But once those blue eggs crack
And tiny beaks appear,
Keeping hunger satisfied
Will be her only fear.

Comes summer time when all her brood
Will fly away alone,
She'll say, "A job well done, Old Girl",
Now peace in "Home Sweet Home!"

# DEAR BIRDIE

Hey little birdie in the tree,
Won't you please come down to me?
I have some seeds just for your food -
My Mom says that you think they're good.

I'm holding my hands so very still
So you can land now, if you will.
Why is it that you won't come near?
Is there something that you fear?

Maybe you're frightened by my cat!
I guess I never thought of that.
No wonder that you stay up high -
There are no kitties in the sky.

# GARDEN WALK

My Grandma took me for a walk
Down through some garden lanes.
She said she'd show me flowers
And teach me all their names.

I found it most amazing as she pointed out some things -
Like a Bird of Paradise that had no song or wings.
There was Snow On the Mountain, but the sun was shining bright,
And some big Japanese Lanterns, but I didn't see a light.

We passed some Weeping Willows, but I couldn't hear them cry.
Then she saw Pussy Willows, but there were no cats close by.
She saw both Hens and Chickens, but there were not any eggs.
Next she saw a Lady slipper, but I could not see her legs.

She pointed at a Spider Plant, but said it didn't crawl
And then she mentioned Bleeding Hearts - I didn't like that at all.
She said she saw some Bluebells, but I didn't hear them ring -
Oh our walk into the garden was one big confusing thing.

# CIRCUS CLOUDS

As I sat in my yard one day
And looked up in the sky,
It seems I saw a big parade
Of cloud friends passing by.

I saw a lion roaring -
Then a monkey with a grin.
A duck came floating by next
And a fish with one big fin.

A camel with two great big humps
Was marching 'cross the sky;
Then a fancy fluffy poodle
With a big bow as a tie.

I turned my head from side to side,
Yet still my friends rolled by.
Oh what a treat to lay and watch
A circus in the sky.

28

# SUNNY SUNFLOWERS

It's wondrous to me how the Sunflowers
All turn to face Mr. Sun.
It's like they all know he's their leader
And they'll all join together for fun.
Their big yellow faces are smiling
As they do dances and curtsy and bow,
And if they don't know how to do them,
The winds will show all of them how.

When their big yellow faces turn into black seeds,
They know they will still do some good.
For when all of their dancing is over, you see,
They soon become great yummy food.

# THE DANDY DANDELION

Most flowers grow in gardens,
But there's one that's much too wild.
It doesn't stay in fences,
And it's loved by every child.

Some people say it's just a weed,
But never me, for sure,
'Cause it's a Dandelion -
One that doesn't even roar.

Kids can always pick them
And grownups don't get mad,
And if a lawn has none at all,
I'd think it must feel sad.

They stay a pretty yellow,
And even though they're tough -
They soon change to a fluffy ball
And are gone with a puff.

# MY HOME

How I love our cozy house!
I know that if I was a mouse
I'd love to come and stay and be
A part of my dear family.

Of course I'd have to run and hide
Whenever mother came inside.
I don't think that she'd really care
To see me running up the stair.

Where would I hide from Jack, our cat?
I'd really have to think on that.
Perhaps it's best to just be me
And stay home, where I like to be.

# DROWSY TIMES

When Mommy tucks me in my bed I
close my eyes real tight
To shut out all the darkness
And find pictures in the night.

I see pretty little ladies dressed
Like flowers dancing by,
And kitty cats and bunnies
Softly brush against my eye.

Then stardust starts a falling
From the heavens high above
And covers me with softness
Sweet as Mom and Daddy's love.

Then the pictures get all fuzzy
And start sinking down so deep
That before I can catch them again
I find I'm fast asleep.

# WIND SONGS

There's a voice in the wind that reaches to the sky.
It puffs up the clouds and sometimes makes them cry.

It sings happy songs when the sun shines so high,
Then as the sun sets, it slows down to a sigh.

It whistles through trees and sings into night,
Then hums lullabies until dawn brings new light.

The moon makes it whisper to almost a hush,
Then it's voice rises up as sunrise sends it's blush.

The voice is a gift sent from heaven above.
The spirit of God comes to us, with His love.

# THE SCENE TO BE SEEN

I thought I looked at nothingness-
just grass, some trees and sky,
but as I looked more closely,
some new things caught my eye.

A black V high up in the blue
grew closer, then I knew
a flock of geese were flying North
where I was going too.

I heard a rustle in the grass
and saw a feather ball-
I spotted a ruffed grouse
that was about to rise up tall.

It flew up quickly with a swoosh
and as it soared, I knew
another visitor close by
had been somewhat startled too,

A deer that had been standing still
behind a cedar tree
bolted out and ran across,
not far in front of me.

As he ran, a pheasant was
flushed out and flew up too.
Now what more did I see as I
turned my eyes up to the blue?

An eagle soared in circles up so high
I almost missed it,
and then a bee buzzed by my face,
So close I could have kissed it.

It landed on a flower that was
down low by my feet.
By now I really wondered what
there would be next to meet.

I then knelt down and
brushed my fingers near the ground
and found some sand hills filled with
busy ants all going round.

A spider walked across one hill
and found his web close by
and waited patiently and watched,
just looking for a fly.

A gopher ran across the field
heading for his hole.
I thought I saw it, but surprise,
out popped a dark gray mole.

I started walking-
It was time to get back to the road,
then saw a snake that seemed to show
great interest in a toad.

I know I learned a lesson as I
thought about this scene,
for I know that it was special,
better than any dream.

Whenever I may stop now
and ask someone what they see,
I'd know if they are special,
or if they were just like me ---

Who looked and saw, but didn't see --
what lessons can be learned
if only we can take the time to see,
scenes can be turned.

Nature does much more than
paint pictures with a brush,
it gives animation
to every reed and rush.

So take the extra moment to find movement,
it's our duty -
for nature tries to teach us
"OPEN UP YOUR EYES TO BEAUTY".

www.ingramcontent.com/pod-product-compliance
Lightning Source LLC
Chambersburg PA
CBHW041434120626
46547CB00002B/208